TRAMPS AND TRIUMPHS

OF THE

SECOND IOWA INFANTRY

BRIEFLY SKETCHED

BY

JOHN T. BELL
LIEUT. COL. "C"

Original Text Unaltered. Reprinted with Footnotes and Drawings

BETHEL PUBLISHERS
P. O. Box 1134
Darien, Connecticut 06820

ISBN 978-0-941136-11-2

To my Old Comrades, Greeting:

I am invited to attend at Ottumwa, Iowa, next month, a reunion of the regiment we all loved so well, and as my contribution to an occasion which will doubtless be a pleasant episode in our lives, I have gathered up a series of sketches, published not long since in the *Omaha Bee,* and present them to you in this form as a reminder of days and events of a period when our nation was "making history."

THE AUTHOR

Table of Contents

INTRODUCTION

The nearly forgotten story of the Second Iowa Infantry is one of the most stirring chapters in the annals of Iowa and the Civil War. The regiment was the first enlisted in the state for three years' service in that tragic conflict a century ago, and the nine hundred eighty-nine volunteers mustered into its rank were the first Iowa troops to take the field in June, 1861. Fully two thousand men fought and died in the service of this gallant regiment before the end of the war. Nearly half of them succumbed to exposure and disease or fell in a score of bitter battles.

Few regiments of Civil War volunteers had a more notable battle record. The men of the Second Iowa led Grant's victorious charge on Fort Donelson in February, 1862, to give the North its first good news of the war; they fought stubbornly in the "Hornet's Nest" at the bloody battle of Shiloh, and suffered nearly one-third of their 346 officers and men killed or wounded in helping to repulse the determined Confederate attack at Corinth, Mississippi, in October.

Greatly reduced in numbers, the regiment took part in the Atlanta campaign in the summer of 1864, participated in Sherman's famed "March to the Sea," and was part of the Grand Army of the West, which crossed the rivers and swamps of the Carolinas to force the surrender of Confederate General Joseph E. Johnston's Army of Tennessee near Raleigh on April 26, 1865, seventeen days after Appomattox.

The survivors of the Second Iowa returned to their homes and families in July, 1865, having endured their full share of the misery and horror of the war in the west. Their memorable experiences and impressions are vividly recounted in this centennial edition of *Tramps and Triumphs of the Second Iowa Infantry*. The brief but valuable recollections of Lt. John T. Bell provide one of the few remaining original sources of a fighting regiment of Civil War volunteers. A veteran of all its major marches, battles and campaigns, the personal history of this young soldier is a very human and moving document.

Lieutenant Bell rose from the ranks to company commander after joining the Second Iowa Infantry at St. Louis in December, 1861. The nineteen-year-old youth somehow escaped the shot and shell of Fort Donelson, Shiloh and Corinth. He studied shorthand while in garrison and served as a military court reporter, which is apparent in his concise, accurate sketches. He served on a number of newspapers after the war, was official stenographer of the Nebraska District Court at Omaha, later dealt in real estate in California, and died in Seattle, Washington, Dec. 26, 1918.

Tramps and Triumphs of the Second Iowa Infantry was originally prepared as a series of newspaper articles for the *Omaha Bee* in 1886. Bell had them printed in a small booklet for the third annual reunion of his old regiment at Ottumwa, Iowa, October 5 and 6, 1886. Long out of print, it is an interesting and useful contribution to the neglected history of Iowa's significant role in the Civil War.

I. FLEMING FRAKER, JR.
Iowa State Department of History & Archives, March 21, 1961.

CHAPTER I

The Enlistment—Guarding Prisoners—
The Battle of Fort Donelson.

In the fall of 1861, a party of five of us left Omaha for the purpose of enlisting in the army. We reached St. Joe by water on the steamer "Omaha" and were sworn in but assigned to no particular regiment. Thence we went to St. Louis and soon found ourselves quartered in Benton Barracks, previously and since used as the St. Louis fair grounds. Here two of our number joined a regiment of Iowa cavalry, two of us drifted into company "C" of the Second Iowa Infantry, and the fifth member of our party we lost sight of as a soldier.[1]

The Second Infantry was the first three-years' regiment mustered into the service from the state of Iowa, and its first field officers all became generals within a short time, namely the following: Colonel Samuel R. Curtis, Lieutenant Colonel James M. Tuttle, and Major M. M. Crocker.[2]

It remained in the army until the close of the war, re-enlisting at Pulaski, Tenn., in December, 1863, for another term of three years. The buildings occupied as barracks at St. Louis were one-story

Brigadier General Samuel R. Curtis

The Capital Guard of Des Moines, Iowa, departing for the seat of war. Sketched by M. H. Bishard.

frames, cheaply constructed, surrounding three sides of a large square which was used for parade and drill purposes. The quarters were comfortable enough, however, but the tedium of the drill and confinement of a soldier's life when first entered upon is wearing beyond all comparison, except it be with that of the life of a penitentiary convict. I remember that I, at this period of my military career, used to walk up and down on the parade ground wondering, "Can I endure three long years of this?" and the only comfort to be found in the situation was the reflection that the war might not last so long, in which case a discharge would come sooner. I was a green boy who had had but little experience in being away from home, slow to make acquaintances, and lonesome to the last degree.[3]

December 23rd, 1861, we are ordered down into the city to take charge of a body of 1,300 prisoners who had been recently captured in the interior of Missouri, while on the way to join Sterling Price. McDowell's medical college, corner

Fort Donelson, Tennessee, in a view looking upstream along the Cumberland River. The Second Iowa left its boat in this vicinity—out of range of the fort's water batteries—and marched inland to its position in the rear of the fort, beyond the hill in the right distance. There it made its famous assault.

of Gratiot and Eighth Streets, whose owner had sought service in the rebel army, had been seized by the government and converted into a prison, a row of brick buildings on the east side of Eighth Street, directly opposite the college, being fitted up as quarters for our regiment. That night I stood guard duty for the first time in my life, and was stationed in front of a window with instructions to shoot any one attempting to get out of that aperture. Fortunately my fears that there will be a sudden and uncontrollable desire on the part of the entire outfit to endeavor to escape by means of that particular window and on that particular occasion prove unfounded, and I am not required to bathe my hands in the blood of my fellows at any time during the long night.

Our service here was quite pleasant, though we were on guard duty every other day. We escaped drill, however. Our rations were abundant, and we took great interest in our regular evening dress parade, which was held on Eighth Street, just south of Gratiot. The regiment was one of the best drilled in the army, had a splendid brass band and superior

Brigadier General James M. Tuttle.

martial music, and these parades attracted crowds of visitors, and much favorable comment on the part of the St. Louis press. On one of these occasions a union lady, who lived directly in front of the position occupied by the regiment when on parade, presented us with a beautiful wreath. It was carried out to Colonel Tuttle by the bright little daughter of the donor, as he stood in front of the centre of the line, the command standing at "parade rest." The colonel directed her to carry it to the color-bearer (Harry Doolittle, whose blood stained the snow at Fort Donelson one week later, as it poured from four wounds made by rebel bullets). The silken flag is lowered, the little girl places the wreath upon the spearhead of the flagstaff, the colors are raised, a burst of music by the band, and the happy child runs swiftly to her mother, while the regiment returns to quarters.

February 7th, 1862, we receive the news of the capture of Fort Henry, whereat there is great rejoicing, and the following day brings with it marching orders from General Halleck, department commander.[4] On February 9th, we escort to a steamer the prisoners we have been guarding, and as the boat swings off into the stream to carry them to Alton, Ill., where they are to be confined in the old penitentiary building, they give three rousing cheers for Jeff Davis, and then three, quite as hearty, for the Second Iowa. The next day we march down the river and take passage on the T. H. McGill, under very disagreeable circumstances.

When we took charge of McDowell's college we found stored away in the attic a large and valuable museum. It was supposed that this museum was fully protected from damage, but a few of our men broke into the room and injured it to some extent, just as our marching orders were issued. This coming to the knowledge of General Halleck, he disgraced the entire regiment by directing that we should march through the streets on our way to the steamer, without music and with our colors furled.

This act of injustice excited a feeling of resentment on the part of the regiment, intensified by General Halleck's subsequent ill-treatment of General Grant after the battle of Donelson, which resulted in our utter inability to appreciate General Halleck in after years as a military man to the degree that, possibly, he deserved.

The evening of February 10th finds us steaming down the Mississippi to Cairo, where we pass into the Ohio. At Cairo we find collected quite a flotilla of gun boats, some of which had participated in the capture of Fort Henry, under command of Foote, and an immense fleet of steamers, with little tugs flying here and there, the personification of fussy importance out of all proportion to their size. At Mound City, a few miles above, we pass large yards where other gun boats are being constructed, adding to the busy appearance of the scene. Our stop at Cairo is short, and in due course of time we find ourselves in the Cumberland, and during the night of February 13th tie up on the right bank of that river a few miles below Fort Donelson, which was then being invested by the Union forces, under command of General Grant.[5]

Leaving the steamer at 3 o'clock in the morning of the 14th, we marched four miles over villainous roads and came to the Union forces investing the fort, stacking arms near General C. F. Smith's camp fire, and while waiting orders listened for the first time to the firing of contending forces, then confined entirely to the skirmish line.[6] Occasionally a man would be brought back to the rear with blood upon his clothing, showing that he had been struck by a rebel sharpshooter from within the line of yellow clay works, of which we caught glimpses through the woods. While here, we saw General Grant for the first time, as he rode up and held a conference with General Smith, then mounted the yellow horse we became so familiar with afterwards, and passed off to the extreme left of the line.

At 2 o'clock, our regiment deployed as skirmishers and remained on this duty until dark, when we were withdrawn to the rear where we built fires in a sheltered ravine and tried to make out supper with such materials as we had with us, though we were traveling light, with the exception of an extra weight in the way of cartridges. We had left our blankets on the boat, and as we had no tents, suffered greatly with the cold during the night, the ground being covered with snow. As our rations consisted wholly of hard bread, some of us started off foraging early the next morning and "raised" a few chickens and some pork, which we boiled in a pot "borrowed" off the people who furnished the provender.

We lounge around during the forenoon awaiting orders, and some of the boys amuse themselves cutting down young hickory saplings. As George Howell handed to a comrade the ax he had just used, he said, "That is the first tree I ever cut down in my life," and immediately added, "and it will be the last." "What do you mean?" was asked. "I will be a dead man before the sun sets this evening," he replied.[7] At 2 o'clock, General Smith, to whose division we had been assigned, rides down to our position on the extreme left of the line, holds a short conversation with Colonel Tuttle, and then the order "fall in!" is heard.[8]

The regiment is formed behind our stacked muskets, the command "take arms!" given, the line is dressed right and left on the colors, the colonel explains that we are to charge on the enemy's breastworks and take them at the point of the bayonet, particular instructions being given that not a shot is to be fired until we are inside the works; the left wing of the regiment to go in advance under command of Colonel Tuttle, the right to follow as a support under Lt.Colonel B. Bakers.[9]

Our first line of battle thus formed, the left wing (which includes our company) with the colors, moves forward, the right a short distance to the rear. We cross an open meadow, then a gully, tear down and clamber over a rail fence, and

Pittsburg Landing, Tennessee, is a narrow gap in the bluffs along the Tennessee River. In the woods and fields about the landing was fought the Battle of Shiloh.

commence the ascent of a hill covered with abattis, or fallen trees. The line is well preserved, considering the nature of the obstructions, and thus far not a shot has been fired by the enemy. On we go, when suddenly we reach a point on the hill where a full view is obtained of the rebel rifle pits in front and as far as we can see to the right and left of us.

"Crash!" and the yellow clay of the pits is covered by a flame of fire which leaps from the rifles of the Mississippians and Tennes-seeans, by whom they are manned, and who are evidently anticipating an assault. The volley passes over our heads, cutting twigs and limbs off the trees. We give a hearty cheer and rush forward, and then the shots of the enemy begin to tell. I feel myself crowded off to the right, and hear my comrade on the left exclaim, "Howell, what are you doing here?" and turn to find that George Howell is crowding forward into the front rank. For an instant I see him, a round, red spot in his forehead, and he falls dead as a bullet crashes through his brain. Our captain, Slaymaker, falls, and as some

7

of the boys stop to help him he cries, "Go on! go on! don't stop for me," and never speaks again.[10]

The first lieutenant drops with a dreadful wound in the leg;[11] the second lieutenant is wounded;[12] Harry Doolittle, the color-bearer, receives four wounds instantaneously and the flag is stretched upon the ground; it is raised by Corporal Page, who is shot dead; Corporal Churcher then takes the colors and has his arm broken and is succeeded by Corporal Twombly, who is knocked down by a spent ball but jumps up and carries the colors to the close of the engagement.[13] Colonel Tuttle is severely injured.[14] Lieutenant Colonel Baker has his hand grazed by a bullet; Major Chipman is dangerously wounded,[15] and Captains Slaymaker and Clotman and Lieutenant Harper are killed.

We have but two hundred yards to go after receiving the first fire of the enemy before we reach their works and capture them at the point of the bayonet. This distance is made at double-quick time, yet in doing it our company of not over seventy men incurs a loss of twenty-six killed and wounded.

We have passed through the dreadful ordeal without firing a shot, but when the earthworks are gained and the enemy in full retreat to a second line of entrenchments, our balls fall thick and fast and do great execution. We continue the advance a considerable distance, but the rebels rally in force behind the second line of works, which are supplied with artillery much heavier than those we have captured, and we are ordered to return and hold what we have gained at such fearful cost.

Reinforcements are rushed up the hill, batteries placed in position, orders given us to hold that line at all hazards. It was a bitter cold night and we had no blankets. We tried to build fires, but as the light flashed up it drew the attention of the rebel artillery to our exact locality, and they rattled shell in among us so that we preferred to risk freezing to death and extinguished the fires. Inside the main line of fortifications, we could hear the cries and groans of the rebel wounded as they were being picked up and conveyed to the hospitals.

A portion of the "Hornets' Nest" line in the Battle of Shiloh. Five Iowa regiments, including the Second Iowa, fought in this line throughout the day, April 6, 1862, delaying the advance of the Confederate force toward Pittsburg Landing. Union reinforcements arrived during the night, and the following day the Southerners were driven from the field.

Towards daylight, we heard bugle calls and moving of rebel artillery and fully expected an attempt would be made to regain the line we then occupied. As the light became clearer, we saw a group of men standing on the main line of works, and two men were seen to come towards us with a white flag. Colonel Baker, accompanied by two or three officers, went out to meet them. The flag was carried by a darkey, the other person being a white officer, who brought from General Buckner a note proposing the appointment of commissioners to agree upon terms for the surrender of the rebel forces and suggesting an armistice until noon for that purpose. This note was sent by Colonel Baker to General Grant, to which the latter replied with his famous "unconditional surrender" proposition, which was soon accepted, and Fort Donelson, with thirteen thousand prisoners, forty pieces of siege artillery, and about twenty thousand stand of small arms, was ours. "Glory enough for one day."[16] As the first lodgment in the enemy's works was made by our regiment, we, by order of General Smith, marched into the main fortifications at the head of the Union forces, and the flag of the Second Iowa Infantry, riddled with bullets and stained with the blood of the men who had carried it on the preceding day, was the first to float from the rebel flagstaff.

The following dispatch was sent to Adjutant-General N. B. Baker at Des Moines, by General Halleck, department commander, under date February 19th: "The Second Iowa Infantry proved themselves the bravest of the brave. They had the honor of leading the column which entered Fort Donelson."[17]

How one feels under fire has been the subject of many articles. There is no doubt that in making a charge there is less strain on the soldier's nerves, though his comrades are being shot down all around him, than in an engagement where he is compelled to lie still and suffer the enemy's fire, as was the case with our regiment at Shiloh. There we had ninety-seven men killed and wounded, as we lay without firing a shot in the "Old Road" at the point designated by the confederates as the "Hornet's Nest."

I remember the most important impression made upon my mind in the intense excitement of the charge at Donelson was a feeling of personal degradation on seeing our flag spread out on the ground. It was no longer a combination of stripes and stars in silken texture, but the vital personification of human liberty battling for its own life, and its downfall,

Picket duty was lonely at night.

though but temporary, seemed the triumph of wrong, injustice and oppression.

The "zip" of the rifle balls have a peculiar stinging sound, and the shriek of bursting shells causes one to dodge instinctively, but I think that each soldier is impressed with the belief that he will not be struck, the dominant desire of his mind being to rush forward and carry the place by assault. It is a remarkable fact that in nearly every instance when a man is struck he impulsively exclaims. "Oh Lord!" "Oh, my God!" or in some similar language addresses his Maker, especially if the wound is mortal. A feeling of intense hatred of the enemy possesses him as the charge is made, and he sees his comrades falling about him, and he is carried away with a wild desire to kill and slay in turn. For the moment, those opposing him are not human beings but devils and demons whom it is his duty to slaughter without mercy.

CHAPTER II

In Camp at Shiloh—The Battle and Halleck's Siege—The Battle of Corinth.

In a few days after the surrender of Donelson we found ourselves quartered in log cabins which had been built by the confederate forces. They were warmed by means of fireplaces constructed of sticks and clay and did not throw out much heat. As only those who could secure a position close to the fire could keep comfortable, there was a general desire to obtain "front seats," and the successful ones were apt to form a "close corporation" and hold their advantage.

One cold day Billy McAllister, of company "B," after a vain effort to break into the circle surrounding the fire in his cabin, suddenly threw a big shell into the fire-place, yelled "a shell in the fire! a shell in the fire!" and as the boys rushed from the building pellmell, to avoid the explosion, coolly appropriated a good seat and then called out to his badly frightened comrades, "come back, boys, she ain't loaded!"

Here we were visited by many people from the north. Governor Kirkwood, of Iowa, made us a speech, telling us that "the backbone of the rebellion was broken," that the war was nearly over and that we would all be home by the following Fourth of July.[18]

Among the arms surrendered were knives of tremendous size, built after the general design of a bowie but much larger, which had formed part of the equipment of the "Texas Tigers." Many of these knives and similar trophies were picked up by the boys immediately after the battle and considerable wealth secured by their sale to our northern visi-

Fighting in Battery Robinett, a scene witnessed by the Second Iowa during the Battle of Corinth, Mississippi.

tors.[19] At Donelson I drew on my clothing account a heavy double blanket which has been in constant service since, twenty-five years, and from appearances will last another twenty-five years, thus proving that all army contractors were not swindlers.

March 6th, 1862, we left Donelson, camping that night near some old iron furnaces, said to be the property of John Bell, of Tennessee, and the next day pitched our tents on the bank of the Tennessee river, at a place we called Metal Landing on account of the immense quantities of pig-iron found piled up there awaiting shipment. Here we suffered for food for the first time, the soldiers stealing the corn fed to the mules unless the teamsters stood guard over the feeding animals.

On the 12th of March, we embarked on the "Champion No. Four" and proceeded up the river, and after a good deal of steaming up and down past a long line of heavily loaded boats, finally on the 9th disembarked at Shiloh, or Pittsburg Landing.[20] While our boat was tied up and we were still on board, a soldier belonging to the Seventh Iowa, on a steamer a couple of hundred yards farther up stream, fell off the crowded hurricane deck and was swept down past us by the swift current. He had on a heavy overcoat and was encumbered with belt, cartridge box and bayonet, but managed to keep afloat quite a distance.

The cry was heard "man overboard!" and the deck hands on our steamer hurriedly launched a boat and rowed out to his rescue. As the poor fellow passed us he gave us an imploring look and probably saw the efforts that were being made in his behalf, but the odds were too strong against him. His heavy woolen clothing had absorbed a great weight of water, and he sank in full view of ten thousand men, his hat floating downstream as his body disappeared forever.

Our camp at Shiloh, three-fourths of a mile from the landing, was delightfully located on a handsome meadow, with large forest trees on three sides. A fine spring nearby afforded an abundance of water; rations were plenty, guard and drill duty light and the weather all that could be desired.

We had good wall tents, organized messes to suit ourselves, and the daily arrival of steamers loaded with troops furnished us with variety and excitement. Day after day the lines of soldiers could be seen marching past our camp to take position beyond us in the beautiful forest. We have a grand review on the 3rd of April, when General Grant rides down in front of the line on his yellow charger and is received with much enthusiasm by the soldiers.

Sunday morning, April 6th, as we are out for company inspection, we hear the "long roll" sounded for the first and last time in our entire term of service. Orders are given at once to take two days' rations, and with forty rounds of ammunition in our cartridge boxes and twenty in our haversacks, the regiment forms in line and hurries to the front. Our regiment is a part of W. H. L. Wallace's division, chiefly troops that have been engaged at Donelson. It is nearly two

Misery and disease marched with soldiers in the southern swamps.

miles to the front where Prentiss had been attacked, the outlying regiments being composed principally of soldiers then hearing the crash of battle for the first time, and as we march at "double-quick" to the front, we soon meet stragglers by the hundreds who have left their commands and are breaking for the rear. They advise us to go the other way.

One poor, scared rascal in particular stands by the roadside, throws up his hands and yells: "For God's sake, don't go out there; you will all be killed. Come back! come back!" But we do not "come back," though there are then marching with us men who have looked upon their camp for the last time.

Colonel N. W. Mills

The roads are full of ambulances and heavy six-mule wagons loaded with wounded being taken to the temporary hospitals. Their cries of pain as the teams are rushed along are distressing; the woods swarm with blue coats; batteries are hurried here and there with horses on the gallop; the terrible din of musketry is directly in our front; shells shriek and burst above our heads; the air is thick and heavy with smell of burned powder, and we are in the midst of what proves to be one of the memorable battles of the great war.

We form in line of battle and finally take position in an old road running north and south (if I am not mistaken as to the points of compass), and are ordered to lie down. A rebel battery concealed in the brush in front of our regiment opens on us, and one of our own batteries dashes up and takes position directly behind us and endeavors to silence the rebel guns. Solid shot, grape, canister and bursting shells pass over us in a fearful manner, and here we have eighty-seven men killed and wounded. One of our company threw his foot forward to stop a piece of exploded shell which was thrown towards the line and which he thought had spent its force and instantly his foot is mangled and crushed, so that amputation follows. I am lying so close to Captain Bob Littler that I could touch him by putting out my hand when a shell bursts directly in our front and a jagged piece of iron tears his arm so nearly off that it hangs by a slender bit of flesh and muscle as he jumps to his feet, and crazy with the shock and pain, shouts, "here, boys! here!" and drops to the ground insensible.

A rabbit, trembling with fear, rushes out of the brush, in which the rebel battery is hidden, and snuggles up close to a soldier, his natural terror of man entirely subdued by the dreadful surroundings. Then to the right of the rebel battery we see the confederate flag moving forward, with a long line of men in gray. They are allowed to come within a hundred yards of our troops lying in that old road, then the blue coats rise, thousands of muskets ring out, and the line of gray coats is broken and hurled back. The assault is repeated for the second and third time with such terrible results to the rebels that this locality is now designated by them as "The Hornets' Nest."

Meanwhile the crash of musketry and the roar of artillery at other points of the battlefield have become absolutely appalling. At least 50,000 men are engaged in the dreadful carnage, and the slaughter is frightful. The long day is drawing toward its close; there is quiet in our immediate front, but the firing on our right and left appears to be getting nearer and nearer, and it is evident that our forces are falling back.

We occupy a central position in the long line and are anxiously awaiting an order from General Wallace to shorten up the line by moving to the rear. But General Wallace has given his last command and at that moment lies dead upon the battlefield. Receiving no directions, Colonel Tuttle uses his own judgment, and about 4 o'clock he gives the order "about face!" and we march steadily back; but not an instant too soon, for General Prentiss' division, joining us on the left, is immediately surrounded and captured. We move back in good order, finding the flanks of our division "in the air," entirely disconnected from any other command. To the right

Helping a wounded soldier.

and left through the open woods, we see a long line of union soldiers extending in an oblique direction, falling back towards each other. We are moving at, substantially, right angles to these lines, though not connected with them.

Behind the union forces are seen the rebel regiments following up their advantage and, as our lines converge, securing a complete cross-fire, which proved terribly destructive to our forces.

This, for a brief space, seems to be the position: W.H.L. Wallace's division forming one side of an oblong, facing towards Pittsburg Landing which is, perhaps, two miles distant, while the other two lines, much longer, are at right angles with the river, and approaching each other in good order, with the various regiments plainly discernible by their colors. Our division apparently connects with both these lines at the same moment, there is a shock as the men crowd on each other, a waver, then all discipline is lost, the Union forces break from control and a mad race for the landing and shelter of the gunboats is made, while the confederates with cheers and yells, "follow fast and follow faster."

I soon find myself entirely cut off from my company and hurry along, the rebel bullets doing great execution in the surging mass. Just in front I see a horse standing quietly, his rider having been shot, and I debate in my own mind as to the desirability of mounting that horse when I reach him and thus gain greater speed in escaping, but before I can seize the bridle a man dashes in front of me, evidently bent on the same purpose, when a rifle ball crushes through the back of his head and he pitches forward in the dust. A single gun with full complement of men, gunners sitting in their places, the riders lashing their horses into a gallop, dash by me in splendid style, going towards the landing.

The uniform differs somewhat from the regulation blue, but attracts no particular attention on that score; they press forward and suddenly wheel, dismount, unlimber the gun from the caisson and fire shot and shell as rapidly as they can be served, into the mob of flying men. Then we know that these are rebel, not Federal artillerymen, and though enough Union soldiers rush by them as they coolly load and fire to pick up gun, carriage, caisson and horses and hurl them into the Tennessee, no effort is made to capture the gun or silence the gunners.

It was a brave deed, but the Confederate army was composed of men capable of such acts of heroism, and for four years it excited and fairly earned the admiration of the world. On the hill immediately overlooking the landing, we found a semi-circle of heavy guns that had been hastily placed in position, and as the union soldiers crowded behind the protection thus afforded, the advance of the enemy was stopped by a destructive fire from these guns and those on the gunboats at the landing, which raked the rebel right. The infantry lines were re-formed to some extent and added their assistance, and thus ended the first day's fight at Shiloh.[21]

At sunset General Nelson's division, the advance of Buell's army, which had been on a forced march for Pittsburg Landing, arrived on the opposite side of the river and was rapidly ferried over by steamboats and formed in line of battle in front of our semi-circle of artillery. We were glad of their arrival and to hear that Lew Wallace's division of five thousand fresh troops had reached the battlefield, after a day's time consumed in marching five miles to reach a position, which Wallace had received orders at 8 o'clock a.m. to occupy. As we laid in line that night, completely soaked with the heavy rain which fell (a rain always seemed to follow a battle), we could hear the steady tramp, tramp, of Buell's men as they marched past us and were pushed out to the front.

We had heard of the death of General Sidney Johnston, the rebel commander, and that he had been succeeded by Beauregard, who had sworn to "water his horse in the Tennessee river at the Landing Sunday night, or in hell," and comforted each other with the remark that he had failed in the first part of his proposition, which was a matter of considerable importance to us.

By sunrise of the 7th, the battle was renewed, Buell's command and Lew Wallace's division of Grant's army occupying the front line and assaulting the Confederates, the Union regiments engaged on the 6th being held in reserve and following up as the rebels were driven back at every point. By 4 o'clock in the afternoon, we had regained all the ground lost on the previous day, the enemy was in full retreat for Corinth, Mississippi, some twenty-five miles distant, and we returned to our old camp.

A visit to the battlefield the next day disclosed a horrible sight. In places dead men lay so closely that a person could walk over two acres of ground and not step off the bodies. Details of soldiers were scattered through the woods, gathering the dead together, and in one instance I saw 230 bodies buried in one grave.

Death had come in all imaginable shapes, in one case six of our men having been killed by a cannon ball which passed through the center of a solid oak tree eighteen inches in diameter, behind which they had taken shelter in a line. The man nearest the tree had his head cut off entirely, the second was struck a trifle lower, the third still lower down, and so on as the ball lost its force after passing through the tree. One of our company took from the dead body of a fine-looking, gray-haired Confederate a beautifully written letter, dated at Memphis a few days previous and evidently from his daughter, in which she deplored, in the most touching and tender manner, his absence, but thanked God that a few days more would end his term of enlistment, and then he would return home to leave his family no more.

During the battle of Sunday the woods were fired, and when we regained our outer camps, Monday, found at one point a pile of corn, containing several hundred bushels, gathered with the husks on. Many wounded soldiers crawled to this pile of corn, seeking more comfortable positions, and when the fire swept through the woods and over the corn, they could not get away and were burned to death. At another place Monday afternoon, I found a bright young boy (a Confederate) lying badly wounded on a cot in a tent. Facing him, on another cot alongside his own, sat a dead rebel with wide-staring eyes, and underneath the cot occupied by the boy was the body of a union soldier. By dropping his left hand the boy could touch this body, and by moving his right hand a trifle he could touch the other.

He said: "I was badly wounded yesterday, but managed to get into this abandoned tent and climbed up on this cot. Soon after this man on the other cot crawled in, and just before dark this soldier lying under my cot. They were both hurt worse than I was, but we talked to each other as much as we could for encouragement. Then, along in the night this man on the cot talked very low and weak, and after awhile said he knew he was going to die and bid us good-bye.

I didn't hear anything after that from the man lying under my cot, and it was awful still from that till morning. When daylight came I found that they were both dead, and I have laid here all day hoping someone would come and help me." I saw that he was carried back to a hospital, but never heard whether he recovered or not.

On April 29th, 1862, we began our advance on Corinth, the department commander, General Halleck, taking personal command of the union forces. It was generally understood that General Grant was under a cloud on account of the surprise at Shiloh, which came so near proving a defeat to us, and it was a common thing to see him riding about attended by a single orderly and receiving but little attention from other general officers. Certain it was that the men in the ranks always had confidence in him, and his plain, unassuming manners made him a great favorite with the volunteers, who had no love for the regular army "style," which was rendered especially distasteful to them by Halleck.

How differently these two men were held in public estimation at the close of the war. Halleck, the domineering, pompous martinet, held on to an ornamental position "by the skin of his teeth,"

General James B. Weaver

achieving nothing. Grant, the modest, unassuming soldier, snubbed and disgraced after Donelson and Shiloh by a man who was not worthy of tying his shoes, gained victory after victory on bloody battle fields and became the most famous man of his time.

As we learn better the real history of the war, we see more and more in the character of General Grant to esteem and admire, and his name will live in the hearts of Americans forever as the personification of modesty combined with the highest type of patriotism and military skill.

The advance on Corinth was very slow, indeed, as Halleck covered the earth with fortifications, the army gaining less than a mile a day at times.[22] We occupied just thirty days in this movement, expecting hourly an engagement with Beauregard's army, which we understood was concentrated at Corinth and numbered 60,000. In those days Beauregard was famous, having been chief in command at Bull Run, where our army turned and ran, when, had they held on half an hour longer, the confederates would have done the run-

ning and our forces could have figured in history as the brave pursuers instead of the panic-stricken pursued.

We were, to a considerable degree, afraid of Beauregard in the siege of Corinth, his proclamation about watering his horse in the Tennessee having a flavor of the wild, reckless French warrior about it which led us to believe that he would attempt any desperate achievement. But he proved to be a very mild warrior, indeed, and when Halleck threw up a heavy line of works immediately in front of Corinth, Beauregard improved his splendid railroad facilities to skip out, after a general destruction of stores of great value to the confederacy, and on the morning of Friday, May 30th, 1862, we marched into Corinth, it having been evacuated during the night of the 29th.

The summer following we spent at Corinth with the exception of a few weeks, when we were at Rienzi, Mississippi, under command of General Gordon Granger, to whom we took a dislike, because we were put through brigade drill for two hours daily before breakfast. Early in September the regiment returns to Corinth and becomes a part of the second division of the sixteenth corps, General Dick Oglesby being division commander. Here I was promoted to the rank of eighth corporal. I would have been made ninth, I suppose, but there was no such position, a "high private" ranking next to eighth corporal. It wasn't much of a promotion, and it was considered the correct thing by a certain class of soldiers to sneer at corporals, but I was glad to receive even this small advance in military distinction, as I knew that other promotions would follow if I lived.

The battle of Corinth was fought October 3rd and 4th, 1862, our position being assailed by Price and Van Dorn, with as brave an army as ever shouldered musket. Our division moved out two miles on the morning of the 3rd, the presence of the rebel force in the vicinity being known, and took position in a line of works thrown up by the enemy when we were advancing on Corinth. The rebels formed their lines under shelter of the timber and in front of the second brigade of our

The 2nd Volunteer Infantry spent much of 1863 and 1864 encamped at Corinth, Mississippi.

division, which was on the left of and somewhat detached from our brigade (the first), occupying a line of works at right angles to ours. In their front the timber had been cleared for a considerable distance and the approach was somewhat obstructed by the fallen trees.

Soon the enemy came in plain view, moving across this space, six lines of battle deep, with flags flying, drums beating and fiefs playing. It was a magnificent sight, of which our brigade had unobstructed view. Steadily the lines moved forward without firing a shot until the advance is within three hundred yards of the second brigade, when it is met with a terrible volley of musketry. The first line hesitates a moment, the second comes up, then the third, and then with a yell the entire command rushes forward on double-quick, the second brigade is driven from its position, our flank is turned, and we are falling back to form a new line. We take position on the east side of an old field, about two hundred yards across, lying flat on our faces. All is quiet in our front. Details are made to hurry off and fill the canteens of the various companies.[23]

The sun beats down with terrible force. A battery dashes up and takes position on our left. Just in front of us is an old log cabin, evidently occupied, and afterwards there is a legend in camp to the effect that in the cellar of that old cabin is a poor woman who, alone in the midst of the wild storm of battle, which soon rages and surges about her humble home, passes through that dreadful physical ordeal, which became a part of woman's curse when the first man and woman were driven from the Garden of Eden.

As we wait, the silence grows oppressive. Little birds twitter in the trees about us and mark the only break in the ter-

Washday in the Army.

rible stillness, save the occasional low whispers of the soldiers as they lie quiet, with pale, determined faces, grasping their weapons and oppressed with the conviction that in all probability they will never again see the sunrise. A gray coat is seen here and there, slipping out from the shelter of the forest on the west side of the field, and a moment later a complete skirmish line follows and steals forward, hiding itself as best it can behind old logs, stumps, and other obstructions.

On it comes, quietly but surely and steadily approaching, and then our skirmish line opens fire, and the rebel skirmishers, having disclosed our position, halt, and three minutes later a line of battle marches out of the woods, followed by a second, that by a third, and that by a fourth. The field is crossed at a rush and the air is filled with leaden hail.

We lie still until the enemy is within fifty yards of us, and then the command is given, the long line of blue coats springs up and pours a terrible fire into the confederate forces. The battery on our left does splendid work, muskets are loaded and fired so rapidly that the barrels become heated and the advance of the enemy is checked.

The ammunition of our regiment is exhausted, and we are ordered to lie down and allow a regiment which has been held as our reserve to pass over us. It proves to be the Eighth Wisconsin, and as it pushes forward, "Old Abe," the eagle which made the regiment famous, throws his head out, screeches and flaps his broad wings with excitement as he is borne forward in the midst of the wild turmoil and uproar, his talons clinched about the standard to which he is chained. But the assault was too heavy and our lines were again forced back with great loss.

Noel B. Howard

Colonel Noel B. Howard of the Second Iowa Infantry.

Lieutenant Bing, commanding our company, was killed; Lieutenant Hall severely wounded, Sergeant Speed killed, and many others killed and wounded, the regimental commander, Colonel Baker, and Lieutenant Colonel Mills, being included among those killed.[24]

We fell back slowly through the woods, and night found our lines closely drawn about the town of Corinth, two miles in the rear of our position, in the morning. Whisky was brought out in barrels, the heads knocked in, and the men told to help themselves. It was the general supposition that the place would be captured, and arrangements were made to burn the immense commissary and quartermaster stores collected there.

Our forces were commanded by General Rosecrans, who had been defeated by Van Dorn at Iuka, Mississippi, two weeks previously, and the Union Army had little confidence in his military skill. Not-withstanding the abundance of whisky during the night, few of the men drank to excess. We knew that a big battle would be fought on the morrow, and the men had no disposition to add to their desperate situation by getting drunk. In town, all was uproar and confusion, stores and dwellings were broken open and our colored cooks returned to our bivouac loaded with crackers, cheese, gingersnaps, sardines, canned fruits, etc., as their share of the plunder so easily obtained.

At midnight we fell in line and the regiment marched from the south to the west side of town and took position on a ridge from which the ground gradually sloped to the westward with a considerable open space in front, a portion of which was covered with fallen trees, an abatis formed by the Confederates when they held Corinth, and Halleck was approaching it by slow degrees. At daylight our company is sent out in advance as skirmishers and takes position behind scattering trees about three hundred yards in front of the regiment. It was a beautiful day, and as the sun rose clear and bright it was difficult to believe that two armies of forty thousand men each lay within a short distance of each other even then arranging for battle. To the left, on a commanding point, were batteries Robinette and Phillips, heavy earthworks surrounded by deep ditches and manned by heavy siege guns so trained as to completely sweep the space in front for a great distance and thought to be impregnable. An occasional shot is fired in our front by the rebel skirmishers, in a lazy kind of way, to which we respond in like manner.

The sun rises higher and higher, and we seek shady places, keeping a lookout for developments. At half-past ten there is a stir among the enemy's skirmishers, and the bullets fall around us in a lively fashion. We are sheltered behind scattering trees so that no one is hit.

Five minutes later the cry is heard, "Here they come!" and a line of battle composed of six regiments marches out of the woods directly in front of us— followed by others of equal strength—and moves swiftly towards us. The commands of their officers are plainly heard, and as it was not intended that one company of the Second Iowa should repel an attack by the entire rebel army, we "about face" and fall back, still deployed as skirmishers, on our main line.

"Spit!" "zip!" "bang!" the musket balls fly past us, and our "common" time develops into "quick" and that into double-quick. We pass rapidly up the hill, which seems entirely unoccupied, save by a battery of twelve-pound brass pieces ready for work the instant we have passed behind it.

Just over the crest of the hill we find the ground covered with bluecoats, the main part of the army being concentrated at this point awaiting the attack, the men lying flat on the earth. We run to our proper place in the regiment and drop down, the rebel musket balls cutting the ground all around us. A bullet passes across my hip, tearing a great hole in my coat, and plunges through the body of Private Downs, lying behind me in the rear rank, killing him instantly.

Meanwhile, the enemy has swept up the hill, captured the battery referred to and turned it on us. There is so much confusion and excitement when we rise to our feet that before we can advance the enemy is upon us and we fall back and form a new line five hundred yards in the rear. Here we reorganize and move forward with a cheer, recover the crest of the hill, recapture our battery and drive the enemy back down the slope with terrible slaughter.

Our ammunition is soon exhausted, but an abundant supply is furnished by the cartridge boxes of the dead and wounded lying all about us. Here Charley, who was one of the few who drank too much of the whisky so plentifully dealt out, made his appearance in the company for the first time since the night before, unarmed and demoralized to the last degree. Bursting into tears, he rushed from one comrade to another exclaiming, "Give me a bayonet, while I shoot somebody." A bullet passed through the high hat of Sergeant Harry McNell, and in speaking of it afterwards he said:

"You boys have made fun of my high hat, but you see it has saved my life, for if I had had a low crowned hat on that ball would have gone through my head."

In the meantime, battery Robinette has been stormed by a heavy force which moves across the open space in full view of the position we occupy. No braver or more desperate assault was ever made, and as the shot and shells of our siege guns, accurately trained by months of skillful practice, tore dreadful gaps in the ranks of the enemy, with the only effect of causing them to close up these gaps and press resistlessly forward, apparently as devoid of fear as wooden men, I thought, "These are not human beings; they are devils."

On they go, the ground shaking under our feet with the firing of artillery, pausing not an instant—onward, still onward; they have reached a point so near the earthworks that the big guns cannot be depressed enough to do them harm; they rush pellmell into the ditch, twelve feet deep and fifteen feet across, with sloping banks; they clamber up the further side, capture the position, drive our gunners from their places and turn the big guns against us.

Magnificent daring!—courage unsurpassed in the annals of warfare—but all in vain. Battery Phillips commands Battery Robinette and hurls into it a shower of shot and shell which cannot be withstood, aided by the fire of many field guns which have, in the meantime, been trained upon that band of heroes, and the few remaining alive are forced to surrender. The entire attack has proven a failure, and soon the last rebel flag has disappeared from our front, and we go down among the fallen trees to assist the wounded.

At one point I met a tall confederate coming up the road with one leg hanging helpless and using two old muskets for crutches. The thigh of his left leg had been shattered by an exploded shell, and after receiving directions as to where he could find a surgeon he moved off, the noise of the broken ends of the bones distinctly heard as they were thrown past each other by the swinging limb, refusing all offers of aid from stretcher-bearers.

CHAPTER III

Three Military Executions—The Regiment Re-Enlists—Moving on Atlanta.

———

Following the battle of Corinth came the usual era of demoralization after an engagement. The men lived high on luxuries procured from abandoned sutler stores; clothing, blankets, and all kinds of personal effects could be had for the picking up, and for several days discipline was lax. The union army followed the retreating foe for twenty or thirty miles, capturing a few prisoners and an occasional field piece.[25] An examination of the haversacks of the dead and wounded confederates disclosed the fact that the enemy had been literally fighting for bread, their haversacks generally containing only parched corn.

Returning from the pursuit, our regiment went to Rienzi, Miss., again and was quartered in an Odd Fellows' hall. The rain poured down, there was no way of heating the building, and the weather too cold to get along without fire, so we built campfires outside and took the rain. As for sleeping, our blankets were soaked with water, the floor of the building covered with several inches of mud and the house crowded with men smoking, chewing, spitting and swearing. It was a dismal time.

In a few days we settled down into a camp in the woods. Orderly Sergeant Piepgras, Sergeant Burchill and I secured an old wall tent to ourselves. Half the end was torn out but we managed to patch it up. We carried brick three-quarters of a mile and built a fireplace and chimney. Many trips were required but we hung on and when we finished it one

The Ruins of Atlanta.

evening, lit a fire and gathered around the comfortable hearth in company with a few comrades whom we had invited in, thought we were well repaid for our toil. Early the next morning orders were received to march back to Corinth, and the first was also the last time our fireplace was utilized.

At Corinth, we erected comfortable winter quarters, four of us putting up a log house ten by twelve feet, with a good fireplace at one end, two double bunks, table in one corner, carpeted floor, and canvas-lined walls. We sent north for books and papers, one of the mess "foraged" an old Kirkham's grammar, and we diligently set about self-improvement. Thus passed very pleasantly the winter of 1862-3, varied with an occasional raid into the surrounding country, taking a week or ten days' time. I was promoted to a sergeant's position and thus escaped guard, police and picket duty.

On one of our spasmodical chases after Forrest's cavalry, just as we were about to go into camp, Colonel Weaver [26] observed one of our boys endeavoring to knock a turkey out of a tree at a house on a hillside near the road, and called out, "Come down out of that!" The soldier did not hear the command distinctly, and as he hesitated a moment, one of company "A," marching directly behind the colonel yelled, "The colonel says, 'knock him down out of that,'" whereupon the forager blazed away again with better aim and ran down to rejoin his company, with the consciousness of pleasant duty well performed.

Another of our tramps from Corinth, in February 1863, we christened "the wet march." We left town aboard a freight train, and flattered ourselves we had only a pleasant ride before us, but at the foot of the first upgrade we struck we had to "disembark" and push the wheezy old engine and empty cars up to the level. This was repeated at frequent intervals for nine miles, when we abandoned the train entirely in the midst of a drenching rain, and struck out into a section of country whose chief productions were sassafras brush and yellow clay hills. Soaked to the skin we toiled along for eight miles and then reached a region of swampy land where the water stood several inches deep on the level, and in the streams sometimes striking us about the waist. Thus we marched all day—slip, slip, slip, over the clay hills, and splash, splash, splash through the swamps, our blankets saturated with water and weighing a great many pounds, the hard-tack in our haversacks transferred into a soft dough; sugar and salt melted together and mixed with the strength of our coffee ration, which had soaked through the little canvas bag containing it. A dreary day, but night came at last, and we turned off the road and stacked arms in a pine grove.

The cook of our company commander had picked up a fine goose during the afternoon, which he prepared to cook for supper, and then laid aside for a few moments while he went after more wood for his fire. When he came back the goose had disappeared, and he never saw it again.

But the next morning, after breakfast, Johnny Mills, one of the toughest chaps in the company, remarked, as he threw away a bone that bore a very close resemblance to the hind leg of a goose, and wiped his mouth with the back of his sleeve: "The last thief is the best owner, always,"—with much emphasis on the "always."

During the summer of 1863, many of our men were shot on outpost duty, and it became very dangerous to be assigned to that service. It was conceded that it was being done by parties fully acquainted with our guard lines, and finally the mystery was solved by the capture of one Johnston, a member of company "D," First Alabama cavalry (Union), of which regiment George Spencer, since the war senator from Alabama, was colonel.

Johnston had left the rebel army, joined ours, and after learning the location of our outposts, deserted and organized a squad of guerrillas and put in several weeks' active service in crawling quietly through the woods up to vidette posts and shooting down in cold blood the soldier on duty. He was captured, court-martialed, found guilty and sentenced to be shot.

On the day of his execution the entire force of five thousand infantry, cavalry and artillery, then commanded by

General G. M. Dodge, of Council Bluffs, turned out under arms and formed on three sides of a hollow square, to which the prisoner was borne in an ambulance, sitting on his coffin. The ambulance was preceded by a band with silver instruments, playing a funeral dirge. At the extreme right of the line the ambulance halted, the prisoner alighted and, leaning upon the arm of a chaplain, was marched in front of the command, inside the square. First came the band with its solemn, mournful music; then four men carrying the coffin; then Johnston and the chaplain (and so near the box which was to so soon contain his remains that he could touch it by stretching out his hand); then the guards, and finally the twelve soldiers who were to shoot him, eight bearing muskets loaded with cartridge and ball, and four with blank cartridges, the weapons being loaded by others so that none would know who fired the fatal shots.

As the party marched in slow time in front of our company we could hear the prisoner praying. "God have mercy on my soul, God have pity on me," while the chaplain spoke to him in words of comfort. Reaching the extreme left of the line, the party move at right angles to the right and stop in the center of the open side of the square, where a freshly-dug grave is seen. The coffin is placed near the grave, the guards step to one side, the firing party form in line about ten paces in front of the prisoner who, in company with the chaplain, kneels in front of the coffin while the latter offers a last prayer for mercy for the miserable wretch, himself so cruel and merciless.

At this moment the adjutants of the various regiments read to their respective commands a copy of the proceedings of the court-martial, and then resume their proper places. The chaplain and the prisoner rise; the latter is seated on his coffin; a long white cloth is wrapped about his head completely blindfolding him; the command is given the firing party: "Ready!"—"Aim!"—"Fire!" Twelve muskets ring out, seven balls pierce the deserter's head and body, the white cloth is no longer white but crimson, and the man who had stained his hands with the blood of his fellows had passed to the world beyond. The body was left as it fell until the whole command had marched past it, in order, doubtless, that the fate which military discipline metes out to the deserter might be fully impressed upon the minds of the soldiers.

The fall of 1863 found the division of General G. M. Dodge, which included our regiment, located at Pulaski, Tenn., seventy-five miles south of Nashville, after a hard march of a week or ten days from La Grange, Tenn., to which point we had gone two months previously, from Corinth.[27]

It was a tough tramp for me individually, as I had started out wearing a pair of new boots made to order and fitting like a glove, instead of the broad-soled army shoes so admirably adapted to infantry service. My feet swelled and soon became so painful that I would have gladly thrown the boots away and gone barefoot, but for the fact that the stony roads over which we marched rendered that impossible.

As I hobbled along one day, every step a torture, Johnny Mills bantered me to trade my boots for his nearly worn-out shoes. "I'll do it," said I, "and give you a new pair of shoes in addition if we ever reach a camp where shoes can be drawn." The offer was eagerly accepted and we sat down by the roadside to make the exchange. With much pulling and tugging I managed to get one of my boots off and slipped my bleeding foot into the cool shoe with a sigh of relief and began on the other boot but was interrupted by old Johnny with "Hold on! it's no trade, for I can't get this boot on to save me," and so, with as keen a sense of disappointment as I ever experienced in my life, I surrendered the shoes, pulled on my boot and stumped along to overtake the company.

My manner of marching attracted the attention of quick-witted Dick Gear, who made some funny remarks there at, whereupon a laugh was raised at my expense. "If you were half as badly crippled as he is, Dick, you'd have been riding in an ambulance for the last three days," said my messmate, Sergeant Piepgras, who knew the suffering I had endured from the first day of the march. Then there was another

General Sherman's army enters Savannah, Georgia, after the march from Atlanta.

laugh—not at my expense this time. A few moments later, Dick left his place in the ranks, joined me, and said quietly: "Let me carry your gun for you, John." A little act of thoughtful consideration, but as I write these words, twenty-three years later, my heart is full of tenderness for the memory of the bright-faced lad whom, on a dreadful day of battle near Atlanta the following July, I helped to carry to a sheltered place, a wound in his side from which the blood was fast flowing, and received his dying message to the widowed mother at Cincinnati. When I sent that message, a few days later, I added many words of my own—how her brave boy had met his death, how the service he had rendered his country from the day of his enlistment in May, 1861, had been faithful, patient and efficient; how he had endured hardship and danger without a murmur, and how his cheerful, hopeful disposition and kind heart had fixed his memory forever in the affections of his comrades.

Soon after our arrival at Pulaski one Samuel Davis was captured near our lines with complete plans of our camps concealed on his person. He was tried as a spy, found guilty, and sentenced to be hung. It was shown on the trial that the plans were furnished him by citizens of Pulaski, and he was told that he could save his own life if he would disclose the identity of the parties. This offer was declined, and the erection of a gallows in full view of the jail where he was confined proceeded forthwith.

Several days elapsed while arrangements for the execution were being made and the offer of freedom was several times repeated but each time refused. On the day set for his death, he was brought out to the gallows in an ambulance, seated on his coffin, in company with a chaplain and preceded by a band playing a funeral dirge. We were formed in a hollow square around the gallows, and when the procession arrived one corner of the square opened and the prisoner and chaplain entered with four men carrying the coffin, which was placed at the gallows steps.

Prayer was offered and Davis started up the steps and just then was touched on the shoulder by an officer who for the last time said: "Give the names of the men who furnished you these plans and you will be granted an escort to Bragg's outposts and given your liberty." The boy looked about him. He was only eighteen years old, and life was bright and promising to him. Just overhead, idly swinging back and forth, hung the noose; all around him were soldiers standing in line with muskets gleaming in the bright sunshine; at his feet was a box prepared for his body now pulsing with young and vigorous life; in front were the steps which would lead him to a sudden and disgraceful death, and that death it was in his power to avoid—so easily.

For an instant he hesitated, and then the tempting offer was pushed aside forever. The steps are mounted, the young hero stands on the platform with hands tied behind him, the black hood is slipped over his head, the noose is adjusted, a spring is touched, the drop falls, the body swings and turns violently, then is still-and thus ends a tragedy wherein a smooth-faced boy, without counsel, standing friendless in the midst of enemies, had, with a courage of the highest type, deliberately chosen death to life secured by means he deemed dishonorable. Of just such material was the southern army formed. The execution of this brave lad seemed a dreadful act, but, as General Sherman said to the citizens of Atlanta, "war is a cruelty which cannot be refined."

In the summer of 1862, at Corinth, an orderly sergeant of the Seventh Ills., had an altercation with the colored cook of his captain; the latter took up the quarrel, shots were exchanged and the captain killed by the sergeant who was court-martialed, convicted and sentenced to be hung. The proceedings and findings of the court were sent to President Lincoln for review.

There was great delay in getting returns and, after being confined for many months, the sergeant was returned to his command. In December, 1863, he re-enlisted for another

Union troops entering Columbia, South Carolina.

39

term of service, went north with his company on a sixty days' furlough; returned to Pulaski and resumed his duties as a soldier. It was generally supposed that punishment would never be imposed upon him, as so long a time had passed since he was tried and he was an excellent soldier and a favorite with his comrades, but in April 1864, the proceedings of the court were returned from Washington, approved, the man was taken from a sentry post where he was on duty as picket guard (having been reduced to the ranks in 1862), taken into Pulaski and hung on the gallows on which young Davis was executed a few months previously.

On December 22nd, 1863, a large proportion of our regiment re-enlisted for another term of three years, or during the war, and came north on a furlough, returning to Pulaski in February, 1864, and on the 28th of April we started to Chattanooga to join the army there organizing for the Atlanta campaign. We belonged to the second division of the Sixteenth corps, only one other division of our corps, the Fourth, being in that department. We were soon after assigned to the Fifteenth corps, commanded by Logan.

Sherman's army at that time was composed of two divisions of the Sixteenth corps, commanded by Dodge; the Fifteenth, by Logan; the Seventeenth, by Blair, forming the army of the Tennessee, under the command of McPherson; the Fourth, Fourteenth and Twentieth corps, forming the army of the Cumberland, commanded by Thomas, and the Twenty-third corps, the army of the Ohio, under the command of Schofield.

The Confederates were then strongly entrenched at Dalton, Georgia, commanded by General Joe E. Johnston, and the first movement of Sherman's was to send McPherson off to the right and rear of Dalton through Snake Creek Gap, a plan which was so successfully carried out that the strong fortifications of Johnston's army were rendered useless and the confederates forced to fall back and take up another position. Thus the campaign proceeded for two months, flanking by Sherman on the right and then the left, by rapid marches and a forced evacuation of heavy lines of fortifications and commanding positions, with but little loss to either side.

A fully equipped infantry soldier bears a considerable load, and on a hot day it is very oppressive. His clothes are woolen, and the dark color draws the heat. He carries a musket, canteen of water, cartridge box with forty rounds of ammunition, haversack with from one to five days' rations, knapsack with change of underclothing, writing materials, etc., bayonet, blanket, half of a dog tent, rubber blanket, tin can to boil his coffee in, and, occasionally, he carries also a frying pan. This, however, was only the case with the more provident ones.

When we first struck the pine woods of Georgia we found some difficulty in cooking. A soldier would pound his coffee in his tin can, using his musket barrel as a pestle, pour in water from his canteen and place the can over a few innocent-looking pitch pine sticks, touch a match to them and turn aside to some other duty. Instantly almost the pine is all ablaze and the can is shrouded in a roaring fire several feet high, and the soldier is fortunate if his can is not melted down before he can rescue it.

Twelve miles was considered a day's march but was frequently exceeded, and we have marched thirty-four miles between camps. When on a long tramp it was an aggravation to the infantry men to see a snippy young officer, fresh from the North and attached to some general's staff, dash by on a horse, and it was their custom to yell out, cheerfully, "Grab a root!" "Jump off! jump off!" "Cut the lines if you can't hold your horse!" etc. If he was fitted out with the tremendous cavalry boots which many of them affected, the boys would sing out, "Come up out of those boots; we know you're there, for we see your ears!" In case his pride sought expression in a showy hat with much brass and feather adornment, it would be, "Come down out of that hat; we know you're there, for we see your feet!"

On the Atlanta campaign, General McPherson added to his popularity with his command by never compelling the soldiers to abandon the road to allow himself and staff to pass back and forth along the line of march, but always skirted the road himself, dodging through the woods, dashing across open fields. And when a stream was to be crossed forcing a return to the highway, he would quietly wait and drop in at the rear of a regiment, hurry across and take to the woods again. In passing he would always recognize and return the salutations of the command with that graceful courtesy which so well fitted this prince of soldiers and gentlemen.

CHAPTER IV

Capture of Atlanta—March to the Sea—South Carolina Campaign.

General McPherson's flank movement to the right—through Snake Creek Gap—having proved successful, he was soon after sent on a lengthy forced march to the right again, with a view of effecting a crossing on the Chattahoochie at Sandtown. But we struck General Hardee's corps posted near Dallas, which little old-fashioned town we marched through late in the afternoon, finding the Johnnies hard at work strengthening their position. Of course we halted; it was nearly camping time, and Hardee's corps of the rebel army said, in substance, that we had marched far enough in that direction, and thus we had two excellent reasons for stopping.

The following morning we moved forward in the line of battle until the rebel line was fully developed, and then we began to dig; a line of works was thrown up which we held for about a week, during which time there was considerable fighting. In one of their desperate charges our regiment captured a number of soldiers belonging to the Second Kentucky Infantry, and as we rushed them to the rear they asked the name of the regiment, and when told one of them said "Thunder! They told us we were fighting hundred-day men; why we fought you fellows at Donelson!"

While at La Grange, Tenn., the fall previous, one of our boys went into a back yard to get a drink and found a man sitting in the shade of the house. He inquired as to the regiment the soldier belonged to, and when informed he smiled grimly and said. "I know you; your regiment gave me this at Donelson," holding up his right hand which had been shattered by an ounce ball.

While occupying this line of works at Dallas the enemy made a night attack on us, rousing us from sound sleep at midnight by a tremendous crash of musketry. We had just been relieved from duty on the front line and were sleeping the sleep of tired men when the command was given "fall in! fall in! Leave everything but guns and accouterments." Away we hurried through the dark woods, the left of the regiment almost running over General G. M. Dodge, who was engaged in carrying ammunition to the front.

Reaching the earthworks we laid down and awaited orders. As far as could be seen to the right and left a line of fire raged and rolled while the ground shook under our feet with the dreadful concussion of artillery and small arms. For two long hours this continued, much damage being inflicted on both sides, and then the attack was abandoned.

A crossing of the Chattahoochie was finally made on the 7th of July, Johnston falling back to his last lines of fortifications at Atlanta. His course was strongly condemned at Richmond, and on the 19th he was relieved and Hood placed in command of the rebel army. This change of leaders was hailed with great satisfaction by the union forces, as they had a much higher regard for Johnston's abilities than for those of his successor.

Having been placed in command for the express purpose of fighting, Hood took the offensive at once, attacking Hooker, in our center, on the 20th, and the army of the Tennessee on the following day. He was badly whipped by Hooker, and was finally driven back by McPherson's command on the 21st, after a most desperate assault upon our lines, in which McPherson was killed, which assault would have been entirely successful had it been made twenty minutes earlier.[28]

After this engagement, we were employed night and day in throwing up fortifications, and, to guard against possible surprise, faced these fortifications towards all points of the compass. In front of these lines we dug holes three feet deep and two feet across, and covered them with brush so that they were completely concealed. Much hard work was required to accomplish this, and as the weather was very hot, the boys voted the whole business a humbug and were disposed to make light of that sort of strategy.

They argued (in a sarcastic way) that each hole would catch a Johnny and that all we would have to do would be to go out, thrust a bayonet through the rebs thus secured, throw them over inside our main works, rearrange the brush and wait for another "installment." We posted a man as a look-out, greeting him with the frequent inquiry, "any rebs in the holes?" to which he always returned the discouraging response, "nary reb." It is usual for troops to "fall in" and then march, but in this instance we wanted the enemy to march and then "fall in." On the evening of July 26th, everything was put in readiness for the abandonment of this line, which was the extreme left of the union army then investing Atlanta, and at midnight we moved out quietly, leaving campfires burning. Orders were given in low tones, the little conversation that was held between the men was conducted in whispers and, for the only time during the war, I saw the wheels of the artillery muffled with cloths to prevent making a noise as we passed along the stony roads.

At noon on the 27th we had reached the extreme right of the union army, facing east towards Atlanta. Battery "H" First Missouri artillery took position on the left of our regiment and arranged to throw hot shot into the city, about a mile and a half distant. It was reported that one shot was to be fired every twenty minutes during the night, and the following morning some of us were expressing surprise that this order had not been carried out, when a corporal who had been up half the night on guard duty said that it had been —that three times each hour a solid ball had been thrown into Atlanta by a battery of artillery posted within a stone's throw of where we were then sitting—yet we had slept through the night undisturbed by concussions which could certainly have been heard a distance of fifteen miles. We had been in the midst of cannonading, noise and turmoil so long that we could sleep as quietly (when we got a chance) under these circumstances as though at home with downy beds beneath us. Then began the siege of Atlanta in earnest. Heavy batteries were placed in position, the lines strongly fortified on both sides, and occasionally advanced by the union army until the city was in plain view of the besiegers, and much damage done the buildings by the cannonading. The rebels had a number of sixty-four-pound guns in position, and the shells from these made a terrible noise as they tore through the trees above our heads and exploded far in the rear. The sharp-shooters of the enemy proved a great annoyance to us, doing much damage.

On the skirmish line a man dared not raise his hand above the earthworks, or it would be riddled with balls. I happened to be looking directly at George N———, of Company "B," one day just as he was shot by one of these keen-eyed marksmen; the bullet passed through his face, and as he rose to his feet after receiving the injury the blood gushed forth in five streams, one from the entrance of the ball, one from its exit, one from each nostril, and one from his mouth. The doctors said he could not live.

He was taken to the hospital and finally recovered, though with the loss of an eye, and the personal beauty which had formerly made him one of the noticeable men in the company, had disappeared forever. He had been a model soldier, always winning the premiums offered for the best-drilled and best-equipped soldier in the regiment, and had taken great pride in his record, but this injury broke his spirit. After his discharge on account of the disability, he returned to our old camps at Pulaski, organized a squad of desperadoes which preyed on the community, and was finally pursued and shot by command of the union officer then stationed at Pulaski.

While occupying this skirmish line one evening just before being relieved, Lieutenant Tom Raush, of our company, remarked, "I'll take one more shot before we leave," and turned to point his Spencer rifle through the little port hole which he had been using through the day, but before he could pull the trigger a rebel bullet struck him in the eye and he fell over against a party of half a dozen who had been talking with him, his blood and brains scattering over us, as he gasped a few times and then was still forever. It was so sudden that it seemed impossible to realize that the bright young man, who a moment before had been so full of life and vitality, had spoken his last words on earth and could not be helped by the efforts we made to relieve him.

During the siege, it was with great difficulty that any assistance could be had from our two colored cooks, who had taken position, with a few thousand other darkies, in an abandoned line of works half a mile in the rear. It was the intention for them to come to the front once a day with bean soup and coffee, but Jake and Jim preferred keeping close to their own line of defenses. Jim made some show of courage but Jake was a great coward and did not attempt to disguise the fact.

When they would come to us with supplies Jake would take refuge in our ditch and lay as close to the bank nearest the enemy as he could get, and as a rebel "tar bucket," or "camp kettle" (as the boys termed the huge shells) would crash through the trees, he would turn as white as was possible for so black a darkey, and exclaim, "Laws a massy! Jist look at dat now!" etc., etc.

We tried to shame him, telling him this was a "nigger war," that he ought to fight for his freedom, gain glory on the battlefield, and so on, but to no purpose. He would listen attentively and reply, "Dis ain't no nigger's wah; dis am white man's wah; white man got into it and he can git out best he can widout my help." He said he didn't want any glory in his and that he was a heap better off with his old master in Alabama and didn't want to be free.

September 1st, 1864, Hood abandoned Atlanta to its fate and it was at once occupied by the union forces. After the surrender of Atlanta, our division, now commanded by General John M. Gorse, was stationed at Rome, Georgia. October 5th we are put aboard trains and rushed off to

Allatoona where the confederates under Stuart "Stewit's Ko," as our southern friends pronounced it, had cut the railroad and attacked the garrison in a most desperate fashion. The object of the assault was the capture of the immense store of supplies which had been collected at that point, but proved unsuccessful though great loss was inflicted on both sides. The flag of the Seventh Illinois Infantry showed the marks of 137 bullets after the smoke cleared away. General Corse received a slight wound on the left cheek, a small portion of the ear being clipped off. When General Sherman was shown this injury upon reaching the field a few hours later, he exclaimed, "Thunder! Corse; they came mighty near missing you, didn't they?" It was the signalling at this engagement between Sherman and Corse that gave rise to the song, "Hold the Fort, for I am Coming."[29]

Among the wounded after this battle was a young man belonging to a rebel regiment, who looked so much like a woman that it was reported that he was one, and, in company with about ten thousand others, I went down to the hospital to see him. Naturally his appearance excited much comment, and it was amusing to witness the vehemence with which he denied being a woman, proffering as proof to the contrary the evidence of wounded men lying all around him, belonging to his own regiment, and many of whom, he said, knew him from childhood.

Near the hospital was a long line of wounded men, and along this line passed a couple of surgeons examining the injuries, and tying to the arms of those cases demanding amputation white strips of muslin, which cases would be borne into the amputating room by attendants. Pitiful it was to note the anxious expression of the poor fellows as they watched the movements and heard the comments of these surgeons, and to see the look of despair that marked the fastening to the arm of the significant bit of white.

In the amputating room were half a dozen surgeons with sleeves rolled up and arms and hands bloody with their dreadful work. Blood, blood was everywhere, on the tables,

General Sherman's veterans on Pennsylvania Avenue during the Grand Review in Washington, D.C. at the end of the war. The tattered Second Iowa was one of several Iowa regiments that participated in the triumphant parade.

on the chairs and so thick on the floor that it was difficult to keep one's feet, while at the door lay a pile of human hands, feet, legs and arms that testified to the work already done. I saw a boy of eighteen placed on the table, his trousers leg cut and rolled back, disclosing a bright red spot on the knee cap.

His face was white as a sheet as a surgeon approached him. "Doctor," said he, "are you going to cut off my leg?" He was answered in the affirmative. "Why, I am not badly hurt!" said he; "I walked seventy-five yards after I was shot. Please don't cut off my leg. Just put your hand here and you can feel the bullet; you can take it out easy enough with a probe, and I don't want to hobble through life with only one leg. For God's sake, doctor, don't cut off my leg. I would rather be killed at once; I—"

A saturated handkerchief was passed over his face and the boy dropped back at full length on the table. The limb is amputated above the knee and a few minutes later he is carried into a back room. Soon after I was asked to step into this room and to hold my thumb firmly pressed against the main artery of the boy's leg. The stitches had broken and the blood was flowing freely. I did so, while the surgeon hurried off for assistance, but before his return the patient gave a last gasp and was dead. The kind Father of us all had granted him the death he preferred to hobbling through life on one leg. It was a clear case of incompetency on the part of the surgeon, but it was only one in thousands of a similar character, and hence was deemed of little importance.

November 8th, 1864, we voted for Mr. Lincoln for president for another term and on the 11th burned our quarters and turned our faces southward.[30] We did not know that we were then beginning a tramp of 375 miles, with Savannah as the objective point, for the purpose of proving true Sherman's assertions that the southern confederacy was an egg shell.

The road was packed and crowded with darkies of all shades and colors, ages and sizes, loaded with stolen plunder of as little use to them under the circumstances as would be a diamond to a man starving in the desert—silk dresses, satin vests, broadcloth suits, china cups and saucers, wine glasses, etc., etc. They were fleeing, not "from the wrath to come" but from their masters, and to the frequent inquiry of "Where are you going, uncle?" they would reply, "We's a gwine norf, massa, wid de Linkum sogers."

On the 15th of November we stood on the hill west of Atlanta and saw that city burned to the ground by order of General Sherman. It seemed a cruel thing to destroy in a flash the accumulations of years, and to lay in ashes the homes of thousands who personally had nothing whatever to do with bringing about a war between the north and south.

Pursuing our march, we struck "the sweet potato belt" of Georgia and for a month made sweet potatoes our main article of diet. We stole big kettles and boiled them; hooked frying pans and fried them; roasted them in the ashes and, for a change, ate them raw. There was an abundance of flour, meal, chickens, turkeys, veal, pork, sugar, honey—in fact, everything desirable in the way of supplies was to be had until we reached the coast, and the entire march was after the fashion of a picnic on a large scale.

Immediately north of Savannah we struck a sandy region, producing little, and for a week were hard up for supplies, our food consisting principally of ear corn and rice in the sheaf, with no means of grinding either. Then all the talk was about rations and when they would be supplied and how. Sixty-five thousand men are scattered through the beautiful forests of pine, live oak and magnolia and at nearly starvation's point. Back of us is the desolated country through which we have marched; in front is the enemy and just beyond, floating at anchor, huge sea vessels laden with supplies sent around from New York for Sherman's army, but which cannot be issued to us until either Savannah, on the Savannah river, or Fort M'Allister, at the mouth of the Ogeechee, is captured. Finally General Hazen's brilliant charge on Fort M'Allister is made with entire success, supplies are rushed up the Ogeechee, and the army is saved.

On the night of the 20th of December General Hardee plants two pontoon bridges across the river, which he covers with straw to deaden the noise of evacuation and the following day we enter Savannah, and Gen. Sherman presents to Mr. Lincoln as a Christmas gift, a strongly fortified city, three hundred pieces of artillery and sixteen million dollars worth of cotton.

By noon of December 21, 1864, we are encamped in the suburbs of Savannah, and a few days later are comfortably lodged in shanties built by the boys of material gathered up in the neighborhood. The citizens generally were very friendly, and it was quite evident that they were greatly relieved in having the place quietly abandoned by the confederate army before any damage had been inflicted by cannonading.

Here I received a lieutenant's commission and cheerfully returned to our Uncle Samuel the rifle which I had carried many weary miles (though, as a matter of fact, the miles were never half so weary as I was).[31] On January 28, 1865, we bid farewell to Savannah and start on our march through South

Carolina, crossing the Savannah river at Sister's Ferry. It was in the midst of the rainy season, the country was low and swampy, and many days were occupied in making "corduroy" roads with poles and rails in order to get our heavy wagon trains along. It was a dismal time, but finally we reached a section where an occasional hill was to be seen; the steady rain-pour ceased, the sun made his appearance, sweet potatoes again became our main article of food, and once more life became worth living.

Occasionally General Sherman (familiarly known to us as "Billy" Sherman) would pass us on the march, riding a chestnut horse, whose quick action, small clean head, bright eyes and restless ears proved that, like his master, he possessed pluck and endurance. We had come to the conclusion that we were invincible, and our siege and capture of Atlanta and the march through Georgia and capture of its chief city, certainly warranted such conclusion.

When our advance would be checked it would be but temporarily. Skirmishers would be thrown forward, the ranks closed up, and on we would go with a yell—wading swamps, crossing old fields, and through the woods. Meanwhile, we were living on the fat of the land, and frequently in breaking camp in the morning enough provisions would be left by a single regiment to keep a dozen families supplied for a year.

As we journeyed, refugees, white and black, joined us by the thousands. Ladies who, before the war, had never waited upon themselves, footed it along the roadside for weeks. Some were in carts drawn by a single ox in shafts, some on horseback, some in open wagons, and, here and there in the procession could be seen a family stowed away in a fine carriage, driven by the colored coachman.

It is estimated that 60,000 of these people have joined Sherman's army by the time we reach Fayetteville, N. C., at which point water transportation to the North, via Wilmington, was furnished them by the government. February 16th we arrive in front of Columbia, the beautiful capital of South Carolina. But little opposition is met with and the night of the 17th finds our division and another camped in the city. Wade Hampton's cavalry was the last of the confederate forces to leave the place, and they had attempted to burn a long string of cotton bales which had been piled up in the center of a wide street for the purpose of being destroyed, but the citizens turned out in force and endeavored to save it.

As we marched down this street towards the capitol building, in process of erection, we could see that the cotton had been drenched and the street flooded with water, and to all appearances, the fire entirely subdued. Men, women and children turned out to see us enter the city, and as we marched past the crowded sidewalks whisky was dealt out by the bucketful to soldiers who would drink, evidently with a view of propitiating them.

Meanwhile, a high wind arose during the afternoon and the smoldering fire in the cotton bales was fanned into flames unnoticed in the excitement, and by dark the fire had reached the business houses lining the street. The liquor distributed to the men has excited a desire for more, and the discovery of a distillery near our camps results in scattering ten thousand drunken soldiers through the city, many of whom contributed to the destruction of the place.

A detail of five thousand men is made by order of General Sherman to aid the citizens in putting out the fire, but the five hand engines are entirely insufficient, and it is apparent that the fate of the city which passed the first ordinance of secession—the capital of the one particular state which had always been been too proud and arrogant—was sealed. It was a dreadful scene; hundreds of houses were on fire at once; men swore and women and children screamed and cried with terror; drunken soldiers ran about the streets with blazing torches; the fire engines were manfully worked; soldiers and citizens heartily joined in the effort to subdue the flames as long as there was any hope of success, and long lines of sentries did all in their power to restrain their reckless and desperate comrades. A few years later, I saw the city of Chicago, many times larger than Columbia, destroyed by fire, but the scene

53

did not equal in horrible details that witnessed in the fair Southern city on the night of February 17th, 1865.

We spend two days in destroying railroads in the vicinity of Columbia and then resume our march to the northeast, crossing the North Carolina line on the 8th of March. On this campaign no regard was paid to roads. The army was kept in as compact a form as possible, and, as we carried pontoon bridges, streams too deep for fording could be crossed at almost any point. In fact the rebels burned all the bridges across the large streams. I remember that on one occasion our entire division of, perhaps, six thousand men, marched through a grist mill in operation, crossing the stream on the dam while our teams forded it. The boys said that Sherman intended to march his army through every door-yard on our route.

At Fayetteville, North Carolina, we were told that flour was selling at eight hundred dollars per barrel, and everything else in proportion, prices being based on confederate currency, of course. One North Carolina "cracker" remarked, "Bread corn is pow'ful skate down hyar this hyar year," and we believed him.

On the 21st and 22nd of March is fought Sherman's last battle, at Bentonville, where the rebels under Joe E. Johnston seek to annihilate us.[32] But there is not much annihilation; the left wing of our army, on which the attack is made, hold their ground while the right moves forward on quick time and get in the rear of the enemy, and it is only by skillful maneuvering that Johnston makes his escape to Smithfield, to the northward, though he succeeded in inflicting considerable loss upon Sherman's army. On March 24th, we reach Goldsboro (our objective point), four days less than two months from the date of leaving Savannah.

Here we found rations, clothing, news from the "outer world," and rest, and all these things were welcome. We had marched five hundred miles, through the heart of the enemy's country, and for the last week thousands of the men had hobbled along ragged and sore, with bleeding feet wrapped in pieces of blanket.

CHAPTER V

Foraging in North Carolina—Johnston's Surrender—The Muster-Out.

From March 24 to April 10, 1865, we remain at Goldsboro receiving supplies of clothing and other necessaries, and on the date last named begin our march to Raleigh, the capital of North Carolina, the men carrying eight days' rations in their haversacks and sixty rounds of cartridges. The load is too heavy and to lighten up, blankets, clothing and all kinds of personal effects are thrown away.

Our first day's march is continued until eleven o'clock at night, and on the second we do not go into camp until three o'clock the following morning. April 12, while bivouacked by the roadside waiting for our trains to cross a swamp we hear of the surrender of Lee's army, and the wildest demonstrations of joy are indulged in. We had had reasons before this to believe that the end of the war was near at hand, but now we knew it for a certainty.

April 13, I am detailed to take charge of a brigade forage squad, consisting of fifteen men, including a sergeant and corporal, and for the next ten days life wears rosy hues for us. The detail is made up as the command marches over the slippery clay hills in the midst of a drizzling rain and when completed, we scoot off through the heavy pine woods at right angles to the line of march, which is to the westward.

Finally we strike a road which runs parallel to those occupied by the moving column and, following this, notice a man's tracks, freshly made (the rain having ceased meanwhile), and indulge in much speculation as to who it is that is trudging along ahead of us. The country is thinly settled and we agree that the first farm house we reach of any size will have our party for guests at dinner and as none of us had eaten in a house for over a year, the anticipated repast served as a pleasant discussion.

At 3 o'clock a large white residence with evidences of comfort and abundance is seen on the left of the road. There were several young ladies at the house in addition to the members of the family, and there was a general indication of something out of the common expected by them. To our surprise we were cordially welcomed and before we could proffer a request were told to sit down, that dinner would be on the table in a few moments. We were soon invited into a pleasant dining room where a substantial and well cooked meal was spread.

"But where are the other two men?" inquired the lady of the house, when our squad was seated and it was found there were two extra plates.

"What other two men?" was asked.

"Why, the rest of your party."

We looked at each other in surprise and explained that we were all present and that there were only sixteen of us. She then stated that about two hours before our arrival a Yankee soldier had stopped at the house and told the family to at once set about getting a good dinner for eighteen Yankees who would be along in an hour or so. This explained the footsteps which had excited our curiosity during the day, but who that soldier was, or how he knew anything about us are mysteries unsolved to this hour.

However, we were very grateful for his thoughtful kindness and also glad to know that the family thus forewarned of our approach had improved the time as they did, instead of notifying Wheeler's rebel cavalry, which was in the vicinity and might have easily ambushed and annihilated us.

Our first night out is spent on the magnificent plantation of the famous man of that locality—"Squire Thompson." His colored cooks prepare supper for us but inadvertently use silver forks and spoons in setting the table, and these the boys, likewise inadvertently, "borrow" at the close of the meal. We tell the squire that we are a small band and realize that we are then a good many miles distant from our army; that we know that Wheeler's cavalry is near at hand and suggest that it may be in his mind to send word by some of his darkeys to that distinguished guerrilla that we are temporarily the guests of his fine mansion, but that if he has, and we are attacked during the night, our first act will be to burn that fine mansion over his head.

He expressed surprise that we should have suspected him of such designs—said he was a southern gentleman—a man of honor, and then added the information that he had served in congress several terms. We were disposed to trust him before receiving the last statement but that destroyed our confidence in him, and half our party stood guard until midnight, and the remainder the latter portion of the night. The parting, at a very early hour the next morning, was mutually agreeable—the squire was glad to see us go, and we were thankful that we were alive and able to go.

Squire Woods, a rich neighbor, two miles distant, had the pleasure of our company at breakfast. Thus far our endeavors to convert ourselves into mounted infantry had proven a failure, owing to the lack of "beasts" (as horses are styled in North Carolina).

In response to a suggestion that he might be able to help us out in this regard, Squire Woods said he hadn't a horse or mule on his place, but after breakfast we took the liberty to search, and found seven head concealed in the brush nearby, and at neighboring plantations others were found, so that by noon we were all supplied with horses, saddles and bridles, and had four mules hitched to a big farm wagon loaded with provisions, and another team of mules drawing an old fashioned family carriage similarly loaded, which supplies we turned over to the brigade commissary that night and started out again. It was an exciting life and full of attraction and variety. At times we were twenty miles from our command, and never passed a house without making inquiries as to the whereabouts of the confederate cavalry, which hung on the flanks of Sherman's army from Atlanta to Savannah, thence across South Carolina and North Carolina to Goldsboro, and all along the march west-ward from Goldsboro. One day I was riding alone along a path through the woods and came to a little house, where, in response to my "hello!" an old gentleman walked leisurely out to the gate, wiping a razor on his sleeve.

"Has there been any rebel cavalry around here lately?" I asked.

"W-a-11, yes, there has," he drawled.

"How long since?"

"Not so terrible long sense. A company of Mr. Wheeler's hoss soldiers went down that air road a while ago," he said.

"How long ago?"

"I can't jist tell for sartin as to the time, but them hoss soldiers was at this very gate, and they rid away jist as I commenced a shavin', and now I've jist finished. You mout guess about how long it would take a man to shave, stranger."

I was riding an excellent horse and the abruptness with which we turned and dashed back the way we came and tarried not until we rejoined the squad was very startling to the old gentleman who stood at the gate, continuing to shed information about the hoss soldiers. He may be at that gate yet for all I know, and still talking.

On the 17th of April our party took possession of a grist mill, hauled in all the corn to be found within quite a circuit, and turned out an excellent quality of meal, which we sent in to the brigade. At this time the two armies were encamped a few miles from each other, and the woods were full of confederate soldiers on their way home from Lee's army, with Grant's paroles in their pockets.

While at this mill Dick Jones and I ride out into the country eight miles one afternoon, with a view of spending the night at a farm house, and at dusk, in the midst of a dashing thunder storm, galloped up to the door of a comfortable looking dwelling. An old lady comes out on the porch, and in reply to our question as to whether she will allow us to stay all night says, "well, I suppose you'll stay anyway, whether I say so or not," and orders a colored boy to show us where to put our horses in the barn.

While we are talking we see three men run to the house and take shelter under the porch. In caring for our horses we are careful to get a good idea of the surroundings and to know just where our saddles and bridles are placed, for we agree that as there are three men there, doubtless armed, and only two of us—Dick being armed with a rifle only, and I with a sword that would hardly cut a squash in two—it might be advisable for us to slip out quietly later on and go back to the mill again.

Returning to the house, our uneasiness is increased by the fact that only two men show themselves—the man of the house, a hearty old gentleman over six feet tall and heavy in proportion, and his son-in-law, a young preacher. At the supper table the old gentleman asked us if we had met any of Lee's men since the surrender of Appomatox, and we replied that we had met a good many.

"If you should meet one that had no parole you would capture him and send him to prison up north?" he continued.

We responded that, on the contrary, he would not be molested—that we were glad to see them go home, whether paroled or not.

Returning to the sitting-room, our host attempted to entertain us, but was nervous and excited. He would suddenly get up and leave the room, and then return and apologize, meanwhile exchanging looks with other members of the family, all of which did not tend to create in the minds of Jones and myself that peaceful calm and mental repose which might have been desired. Finally said he, "The reason I asked about Lee's men was, I have a relative who reached home lately from Lee's army, without a parole, and I didn't want him captured, that's all."

Then we knew that the "relative" aforesaid was the third man we had seen on the porch and were convinced that he was concealed nearby. As we talked the old gentleman gained confidence, told us that the relative was his own boy, and that he would bring him into the room if he could depend on our not taking him prisoner. We urged him to bring him in; that instead of his boy being in our power we were in theirs; there were three of them and two of us; that Wheeler's cavalry was encamped near by, while it was eight miles back to our lines.

"That's so," he exclaimed, and the situation evidently struck him in a new light. He left the room at once to return a moment later followed by his "boy," a splendid specimen six feet two inches tall, weighing nearly two hundred pounds, and twenty-nine years of age. We were soon "acquainted," and with the anxiety of the family, and the suspicions of Jones and I with regard to that third man relieved, we passed a delightful evening, or night rather, for it was nearly morning before there was any thought of going to bed.

We found the son a modest, intelligent man, who had seen much service as a cavalry man, and it was pleasant to note the pride the father took in his "boy" as we talked over the events of the war. The returned soldier was out on a scout at the time of Lee's surrender, hence was not paroled—to the great regret of his family, who thought he was therefore liable to capture by our army. I was urged to parole him, and this I undertook to do, albeit I had never seen a parole and doubted my authority, though I did not say so. Pen and ink were produced and the following document evolved:

"I, James Boling, first lieutenant, company "I," Third North Carolina cavalry, do solemnly swear that I will not take up arms against the United States government until I am regularly exchanged. So help me God." To this he signed his name and rank and then followed my own, with the date.

Upon starting back to camp the next morning the lieutenant offered me his sword. He had tendered it when he received his parole, but was told that we would let that matter rest until morning. I wanted that weapon and thought I had a right to it, but in our talk during the night he said much concerning the sword—how he obtained it and the length of time it had been carried by him and where. He was evidently attached to it, and when he handed it to me the next morning, with the belt and trappings, there were tears in his eyes, and his voice shook. The sword was passed back to him. I wouldn't have taken it though the blade had been of gold and the handle studded with diamonds.

On the 14th of April Sherman's army captures another state capital—Raleigh, N. C.—and we march through the city, passing the capitol building, on the steps of which Sherman and his staff are posted. The streets are lined with citizens whose conduct indicates that there is no regret on their part that the place is in the hands of the "enemy," for the ordinance of secession had not been a popular measure with the people of "The Old North State," and for four years the mountains had secreted thousands of loyalists who could not be forced into waging war upon the government of their fathers.

As we marched in columns of companies, keeping step to the music of the national airs, the sight of the grand old flag brought tears to their eyes, and cheers and waving of handkerchiefs gave expression to their greater love for our common country.

Twelve miles west of Raleigh the command halts. It is known to us that negotiations are pending for the surrender of Johnston's army, the propositions being of the most generous character, based upon intimations given General Sherman by President Lincoln a few weeks previous.

Meanwhile, the grandest man this country has ever produced has been foully murdered, and a horrified and outraged nation cry out against the liberal terms Sherman has offered—though they had originated with the great and tender heart that is now stilled forever—and, having been sent to Washington for endorsement, are returned by Mr. Stanton disapproved, and he sends General Grant down to receive the surrender of Johnston's army on terms more in keeping with public sentiment. We are visited in our camps by Grant, but he gives no intimation to General Sherman of his real mission, allowing the latter the full honor of receiving the surrender of the brave army he had first met in the advance on Atlanta, another evidence of the modesty of General Grant and of his high sense of honor and fairness.

April 29, 1865, one year from the day we marched out of our camps at Pulaski, Tenn., on the Atlanta campaign, we started on our last march for Washington, via Richmond, knowing that our days of battle are over, as we have just witnessed the surrender of the last rebel command worthy of being called an army.

It is a happy time, at first as we march through the pine forests of North Carolina and pass the well cultivated plantations where the citizens have filled buckets, tubs and barrels with cool water for the soldiers. Darkeys have come long distances to see us and are wild with joy. One old chap exclaimed that "de whole world has gone by since daylight." Another sang out, "Dar goes my boys! Hurra for dem. Dey clars ebberting before 'em." A woman who was overjoyed with her newly acquired freedom shouted "You uns all is angels from hebben!"

But our tramp to Richmond was a hard one. It was reported that the various corps commanders had laid a wager as to who should reach that city first, and as the weather was exceedingly hot there was much suffering among the men. One day we marched thirty-two miles, and when our company of forty-two men stacked arms at night there were only six in the ranks; the others had dropped out during the day, unable to keep up the terrible pace, and were scattered for miles along the road in the rear.

Before reaching Richmond, hundreds of men in Sherman's army were sunstruck, and in many instances death resulted. I saw men of my own acquaintance, who had gone through battles and dangers, enduring great hardships but surviving them all and living to the end of the war; who had started on our northward march from Raleigh with hearts filled with gladness by thoughts of home and freedom—these men I have seen drop to the ground from the effects of sunstroke, and, with foaming lips and staring eyes writhe in the dust with agony, the victims of a brutal lack of consideration on the part of officers whose only thought should have been to care for these heroes and make light and pleasant this last march, homeward bound, after so many months and years of danger and suffering. Men died on that dreadful journey who had earned the right to see their homes and loved ones again, but were denied that right and murdered by the heartless indifference of corps and division commanders.

The story of the wager may have had no foundation but the fact remains that the march of Sherman's army from the capital of North Carolina to the capital of Virginia in the month of May, 1865, after the war had closed, and when there was no occasion whatever for rapid movement, was a season of terrible suffering to the infantry and the direct cause of the death of scores—to put it with great moderation. From Richmond to Washington City, the march is much easier and is over historical ground.

One night we camp near Hanover court house—a building erected in 1735, forty years before the first gun was fired in the Revolu-tionary War. On May 17th we cross the Rappahannock at Fredericksburg and scan with "military eyes" the battlefield where Burnside was so badly whipped in 1863, and wonder how any man with ability sufficient to command a picket guard could have attacked an enemy so splendidly posted, crossing a considerable stream immediately in front of his position in order to make the assault.

We march past the little church in which General Washington was married (at least so we are told), and on the 20th of May go into camp on the south side of the Potomac, two miles above Alexandria. Two days later the army of the Potomac, neat, trim and tidy, marches past the capitol building, down Pennsylvania avenue and in front of the White House, and the following day Sherman's army, ragged, browned, and as destitute of "trappings" and surplus baggage as could well be imagined, took the same line of march under triumphal arches, past groups containing hundreds of school children singing in chorus—cheered by tens of thousands of people lining the sidewalks, filling doors, windows, and balconies, and covering the roofs of buildings; flowers and bouquets showered upon us from all sides—down in front of the white house where, opposite the bronze statue of Jackson, a large stand has been erected in which are seated President Johnson and his cabinet, Grant, Sherman, Meade, Logan, Howard, and many distinguished military men from foreign countries. "Proud?" I should say so.

Every man marched as though the gaze of that vast assemblage was focused on him individually, and, though his clothing and personal adornment were not much to speak of, the consciousness of soldierly duty well performed at Belmont, Donelson, Shiloh, Corinth, Dalton, Resaca, Dallas, Kennesaw, Atlanta, Allatoona, Milledgeville, Savannah, Columbia, Bentonville, Goldsboro and Raleigh, and the many, many miles that he had tramped between these points, gave a vigor to his body, firmness to his step and brightness to his eye which his better clad brother who passed in review the day previous lacked entirely.

Behind the various divisions came the cooks and camp followers, with camp equipage packed on donkeys and mules. In this train, decked out with ribbons, marched two magnificent oxen, which had been received while the army was at Chattanooga a year before, for beef purposes. They were not needed there, and were driven along on the Atlanta campaign, thence to Savannah and around through the Carolinas, as carefully tended and cared for as two pet kittens. The boys named them "Chattanooga" and "Chickamauga," and it was a matter of congratulation that their behavior on the grand review was all that could be desired.

Another review was witnessed on this occasion by Mr. Bret Harte, which the rest of us saw not, thus:

> I read last night of the grand review
> In Washington's chiefest avenue
> Two hundred thousand men in blue,
> I think they said was the number

'Till I seemed to hear their trampling feet,
The bugle blast and the drum's quick beat,
The clatter of hoofs in the stony street,
The cheers of the people who came to greet,
And the thousand details that to repeat
    Would only my verse encumber
'Till I fell in a reverie, sad and sweet,
And then to a fitful slumber,
When lo! in a vision I seemed to stand
In the lonely capitol. On each hand
Far stretched the portico, dim and grand
Its columns ranged like a martial band
Of sheeted specters, whom some command
    Had called to a last reviewing.
And the streets of the city were white and bare;
No footfall echoed across the square;
But out of the misty midnight air
I heard in the distance a trumpet blare,
And the wandering night-winds seemed to bear
    The sound of a far tattooing.

Then I held my breath with fear and dread,
For into the square with a brazen tread,
There rode a figure whose stately head
O'erlooked the review that morning;
That never bowed from its firm-set seat
When the living column passed its feet,
Yet now rode steadily up the street
To the phantom bugle's warning,
'Till it reached the capitol square, and wheeled,
And there in the moonlight stood revealed
A well known form that in state and field
Had led our patriot sires;
Whose face was turned to the sleeping camp,
Afar through the river's fog and damp,
That showed no flicker, nor waning lamp,
Nor wasted bivouac fires.
And I saw a phantom army come,

With never a sound of fife or drum,
But keeping time to a throbbing hum
Of wailing and lamentation
The martyred heroes of Malvern Hill,
Of Gettysburg and Chancellorsville,
The men whose wasted figures fill
The patriot graves of the nation.

And there came the nameless dead—the men
Who perished in fever swamp and fen,
The slowly starved of the prison-pen;
And, marching beside the others,
Came the dusky martyrs of Pillow's fight,
With limbs enfranchised and bearings bright;
I thought—perhaps 'twas the pale moonlight—
They looked as white as their brothers!

And so all night marched the nation's dead
With never a banner above them spread,
Nor a badge, nor a motto brandished;
No mark—save the bare uncovered head
    Of the silent bronze Reviewer;
With never an arch save the vaulted sky:
With never a flower save those that lie
On the distant graves—for love could buy
No gift that was purer or truer.

So all night long swept the strange array,
So all night till the morning gray
I watched for one who had passed away,
With a reverent awe and wonder,—
Till a blue cap waved in the lengthening line,
And I knew that one who was kin of mine
Had come; and I spake—and lo! that sign
Awakened me from my slumber.

Leaving Washington June 2nd, we reached Louisville, Ky.,
via the Baltimore & Ohio railroad to Parkersburg, Va., and

thence by boat down the Ohio, on both banks of which stream people assembled by the thousands and greeted us as we passed with cheers, waving of handkerchiefs and firing of cannon. Our camp at Louisville is a few miles out from the city and is pleasantly located but we are impatient to be mustered out of the service, and the order to prepare "muster-out rolls" which is received on the 5th of July excites wild demonstrations of joy and there is a general illumination of the camps at night.

Thousands of candles are tied in the tree tops and lighted, bonfires are built beneath and the boys march up and down shouting, singing martial songs and otherwise giving expression to their feelings of delight. July 19th finds the regiment at Davenport, Iowa, when the enlisted men receive their pay and discharge papers. The following day the officers are served likewise, provided they can take an oath in which they call upon all the Holy Evangelists to witness that they owe Uncle Samuel not a cent on account of the guns, ammunition, clothing, camp and garrison equipage and other munitions of war issued the men and for which they are held responsible until relieved by properly made out vouchers. Then we receive our pay and discharges and by sundown of the 20th of July, 1865, cars and steamers are carrying us to the north, south, east and west, and the Second Iowa Veteran Infantry, mustered into the service May 28, 1861, when the rebellion was very young indeed, has ceased to exist.[33]

FOOTNOTES

1. The Second Iowa, under West Point graduate Samuel R. Curtis, who resigned from Congress to become its first colonel, had been ordered into Missouri along with the First and Third Iowa volunteers to help preserve that turbulent border state for the Union cause, embarking from Keokuk, June 13. The regiment rendered valuable service in keeping communications open and in guarding important points in the western and southeastern sections of the state while stationed at St. Joseph and Pilot Knob during much of that summer. Over half the men were sometimes unfit for duty, due to lack of proper medical and sanitary care, and there was need of new recruits upon arriving in camp near St. Louis, Oct. 29, 1861.

2. Curtis, whose home still stands in Keokuk, was made brigadier general in August and put in command of the Army of the South West. He won an important victory in the Battle of Pea Ridge in March 6-8 the following year. Lt. Col. James M. Tuttle succeeded him to lead the regiment into battle at Fort Donelson and command a brigade of Iowa troops at Shiloh. As brigadier general, he had a division at Vicksburg and was honored with the Democratic nomination for governor in 1863. Marcellus M. Crocker was a rising young Des Moines lawyer who had attended West Point but was forced to withdraw because of his health. He recruited Co. D from Polk County, became Lt. Colonel of the regiment, and in October, 1861 was commissioned Colonel of the 13th Iowa. Promoted to brigadier general, his brigade became known as "Crocker's Greyhounds." See Capt. A. A. Stuart, *Iowa Colonels and Regiments,* Des Moines, 1865.

3. John Thomas Bell was a 19-year-old farm youth when he joined Company C of the Second Iowa December 2, 1861. His military record in the Civil War Section of the Nat. Archs. describes him as being 6 feet, 6-inches in height, with dark complexion, grey eyes and brown hair.

4. U. S. Grant at Cairo, Illinois, received permission from General Halleck, department commander at St. Louis, to force the Tennessee and Cumberland rivers into the heart of the

JOHN T. BELL

Confederacy with the support of Flag-Officer Andrew H. Foote's flotilla of gunboats. Fort Henry, on the east bank of the Tennessee, uncompleted, underarmed and partially flooded, surrendered to Grant's army of 15,000 after a short bombardment from gunboats.

5. Fort Donelson, ten miles east of Fort Henry on the Cumberland, was a far stronger post. Feb. 12-13, Grant positioned his army around the 3 miles of outworks as the temperature fell to ten above zero and snow began falling.

6. At 60 years of age, Smith was a veteran, experienced officer whom many regulars regarded as the most capable in the army. He had command of one of Grant's three divisions, including Col. Jacob G. Lauman's brigade of the 2nd, 7th and 14th Iowa, and the 25th Indiana.

7. The Descriptive Book of Company C describes George Washington Howell as 20 years old, 5 ft. 5, light complexion, grey eyes, dark brown hair, cotton Lil batten manufacturer, shot in side.

8. The Confederate garrison of approximately 18,000, poorly provisioned and armed, attempted to break out after three days of intermittent fighting, but failed to push its advantage over McClernand's scattered division. Grant hurried back from a conference with Foote to quickly appraise the situation and ordered Lauman's brigade to assault from the left of his line.

9. James Baker, a Bloomfield attorney, was the first captain of Co. G from Davis County, and he became the third Colonel of the regiment upon the promotion of Tuttle, June 22.

10. Jonathan Smith Slaymaker's last words are quoted in the Company Descriptive book as "Charge boys, charge." Twenty-six, he was elected captain of Company C, October 4, 1861, on the resignation of Jacob DeWitt Brewster.

11. First Lt. Wm. F. Holmes' leg was broken.

12. This was probably Loron Wallace Pierce, slightly wounded in the arm.

13. Twombly later listed all six corporals as being killed or wounded in the charge.

14. A cannon ball struck a log on which he was standing, injuring his leg.

15. Major Chipman recovered to serve as chief of staff to General Curtis, was later brevetted a brigadier general and served as Judge Advocate of the military court which condemned to death the keeper of Andersonville Prison. As adjutant general of the Grand Army of the Republic in 1868, Chipman wrote the general order establishing May 30th as Memorial Day. "Iowan Suggested Memorial Day," Annals of Iowa, Vol. XXXV (July, 1959), p. 64.

16. Estimated at about 14,000. No record of their number was made.

17. The state legislature broke up in a scene of wild jubilation upon receiving the news of Fort Donelson. Described by Charles Aldrich, "The Legislature and Fort Donelson," Iowa Historical Record, Vol. VIII (January, 1892), p. 215.

18. Even Grant felt the Confederacy would collapse from one hard blow until the battle of Shiloh proved him wrong.

19. Most Confederate soldiers carried these knives until they discovered they were excess baggage and discarded them.

20. Chosen as a base of operations against Corinth, a vital rail center.

21. Colonel Baker's report of Shiloh, in which he commanded the Second Iowa, has been lost. Col. Tuttle's report of the battle reads: "We had been in line but a few moments, when the enemy made their appearance, and attacked my left wing (12th and 14th Iowa). They again formed, under cover of a battery, and renewed the attack upon my whole line, but were repulsed as before. A third and fourth time they dashed upon us, but were each time baffled and completely routed. We held our position about six hours, when it became evident that our forces on each side of us had given way so as to give the enemy an opportunity of turning both our flanks." Report of the Adjutant General, Iowa, Vol. II, *State Printer*, Des Moines, 1863, p. 803.

22. Halleck's excessive caution in the advance is reflected in a letter by Corporal Voltaire P. Twombly, May 27, 1862, ". . .I thought I would not write until after the battle, but I have come to the conclusion that it is no use to wait any longer as the impending battle seems as far off as ever. The last four times that we have moved we have thrown up breast works & we will probably have to throw up one or two more lines of works before the grand final .... I was in pickett the day the advance was made. We did not meet with much opposition. Our picketts are continually exchanging shots with those of the enemy but seldom with any effect."

23. Bell seems to have lost and have been charged for a number of canteens at 44 cents each, according to his records.

24. Colonel Baker was mortally wounded on the first day. Lt. Col. Noah Webster Mills took command of the regiment until wounded in the foot the following day. He tragically contracted lock jaw and died eight days later. He wrote in his last moment to his wife whose father, General Hackleman, was also killed at Corinth, "In the army I have tried conscientiously and prayerfully to do my duty; and if I am to die in my youth, I prefer to die as a soldier of my country. To do so as a member of the 2nd Iowa is glorious enough for me." Leonard Brown, *American Patriotism*, Redhead and Wellslager, Des Moines, 1869.

25. Grant was bitterly disappointed at Rosecrans' failure to pursue Van Dorn's broken army.

26. James B. Weaver became the fifth colonel of the regiment. A proud, handsome officer with a good mind, he remained with it until the beginning of the Atlanta campaign in the spring of 1864. Weaver was elected to Congress after the war and twice nominated for president by the Greenback and Populist parties.

27. Major General Grenville M. Dodge of Council Bluffs rendered his greatest service to Grant in building and repairing the railroads to supply and provision the union armies in the west. He later achieved prominence as the builder of the Union Pacific railroad.

28. Bell undoubtedly is referring to the Battle of Atlanta of July 22, 1864. McPherson was killed on that date.

29. The Second Iowa did not arrive at Allatoona until after the battle had ended.

30. Iowa soldiers in the field were permitted to vote by absentee ballot by a special act of the Legislature. 16,844 of their votes went to Lincoln and only 1,183 to McClellan.

31. The original muster roll dates his commission from Jan. 1, 1865.

32. Bentonville was fought March 19-21, 1865.

33. Bell became a prominent and respected citizen after the war. He removed to California in later years where he operated a real estate business at Oakland. He died on Dec. 26, 1918, while visiting a daughter in Seattle.

This map locates the places mentioned in the text.